YOUR KNOWLEDGE HAS VALUE

- We will publish your bachelor's and master's thesis, essays and papers

- Your own eBook and book - sold worldwide in all relevant shops

- Earn money with each sale

Upload your text at www.GRIN.com and publish for free

GRIN ☺

Bibliographic information published by the German National Library:

The German National Library lists this publication in the National Bibliography; detailed bibliographic data are available on the Internet at http://dnb.dnb.de .

Imprint:

Copyright © 2014 GRIN Verlag
Print and binding: Books on Demand GmbH, Norderstedt Germany
ISBN: 9783346017963

This book at GRIN:

https://www.grin.com/document/496875

Showket Ibraheem

An analysis of Fitzgerald's "The Great Gatsby"

GRIN Verlag

GRIN - Your knowledge has value

Since its foundation in 1998, GRIN has specialized in publishing academic texts by students, college teachers and other academics as e-book and printed book. The website www.grin.com is an ideal platform for presenting term papers, final papers, scientific essays, dissertations and specialist books.

Visit us on the internet:

http://www.grin.com/

http://www.facebook.com/grincom

http://www.twitter.com/grin_com

F. Scott Fitzgerald is one of the most recognized figures in American literary and cultural history. His novels and short stories provide some of the best insights into the lifestyles of the rich during America's most prosperous era while at the same time examining major literary themes such as disillusionment, coming of age and the corruption of the American dream. The life of F. Scott Fitzgerald was marked by as much romanticism and tragedy as could be found in his novels and stories. Throughout his life he unsuccessfully battled alcoholism, depression and his inner demons.

Fitzgerald first began working on his third novel in 1922. His initial plan involved a story that took place in Mid-West and New York in 1885. He later reconsidered as he reported to his editor Maxwell Perkins: —*I want to write something new, something extraordinary and beautiful and simple + intricately patterned* (Píchová 12).

Most of Fitzgerald's writing is based on his own experiences. He often got inspired by his surroundings and people in his life. Therefore it is no surprise that his wife Zelda served as the prototype for Daisy and Fitzgerald himself could be identified partially in Nick but also in Gatsby. On the latter he commented: —*He started out as someone I know but at the end he turned into me.* (Burnam 9)

There was another significant event that influenced the story of *The Great Gatsby*. When the family moved from New York to the French Riviera in order to find peace so Scott would be able to finish his novel, Zelda feeling a bit neglected had an affair with a French aviator Edouard Jozan. She ended things immediately after Fitzgerald found out. Some critics argue that this event heavily influenced Fitzgerald and that all his frustration and the loss of certainty of Zelda's love was represented by Gatsby's disillusionment with Daisy and the shattering of his dream. (Stolarek 51)

The Great Gatsby was published in 1925 by Charles Scribner's Sons, a publishing house located in New York. Set in Long Island the novel tells a story of a man whose quest to recapture the past and the woman he loves become ultimately his downfall. The novel begins with the introduction to the narrator. Nick Carraway is a young man from Minnesota who after returning home from the war moves to New York in order to become a bond salesman. Instead of living in the city he chooses to rent a house in the West Egg, unfashionable area where all the newly rich people live. The West Egg is located opposite the more fashionable East Egg. One of Nick's neighbours is a very mysterious man who gave his name to the novel – Jay Gatsby. Every Saturday he throws lavish parties in his huge mansion that even has a private beach. As Nick later finds out everybody is invited.

The heavy use of simile and metaphor also serves as a reflection on the life of the1920s. On one hand there is the East Egg, the symbol of the upper class with its money and the power it bestows upon its holder, on the other hand there is the Valley of ashes which serves as a symbol of the lower middle class and the dull life its inhabitants are living.(Johansson 28)

Fitzgerald also uses the figures of speech to emphasize the contrasts within the novel. The Great Gatsby is rich in contrast. There is the moral corruption of Tom and Daisy against the noble and romantic dream of Gatsby. There are the old traditional family values of the West and the modern way of life of the East. Nick serves as a partially involved narrator and he is clearly torn between all these contrasts. He is personally invested in the story but still able to keep his distance. At least until Gatsby's death when he realizes that he has to choose. No matter how much he might disagree with Gatsby and his quest to repeat the past, he still respects him. Nick feels that it is his obligation to ensure that Gatsby doesn't have to go alone through all of that. He lets himself believe, even if only for a while, what Gatsby believed and feels sympathy for him.

Themes, motifs and symbols play an important part in the story. They point to something deeper which lies within the plot. Because Fitzgerald's style is full of symbols that hold second or even third hidden meaning it is especially important that the reader understands them.

The way the American East and West are presented in *The Great Gatsby* also reinforces the mythical dimension of the novel. In fact, the contrast between the American East and West becomes very significant in explaining the main theme of the novel, which Is the romantic quest of Gatsby.

At the centre of the novel is the vital contrast between America's romantic Western past and the unromantic Eastern present. Both Nick Carraway and Gatsby belong to the West, and both find it difficult to adapt themselves to the way of life in the East. They live in West Egg, which is rather the unfashionable region of Long Island. Tom and Daisy live in East Egg, which is rich, fashionable, and materialistic in sprit. Talking about the Buchanans, Nick Carraway says " why they came East, I don't know." But Tom himself declares, 'Td be a God damned fool to live anywhere else" (20). Tom and Daisy represent the East's callous materialistic spirit and lack of the romantic wonder.

The notion that the flow of history can be arrested, perhaps even reversed, recurs in The Great Gatsby as a consequence of the universal human capacity for regret and the concomitant tendency to wish for something better. Nick Carraway has come East not simply to learn the bond business, but because his wartime experiences have left him restless in his midwestern hometown and because he wishes to make a clean break in his relationship with a woman whom he likes but has no intention of marrying. The predominant traits of Nick's character- patience, honesty, and levelheadedness-derive from his sure senses of history and social position, and yet in the chronology of the story he is first to succumb to the idea that life is subject to continual renewal. Of his roots in time and place he tells us,

The fresh start Nick seeks in the East represents not so much a rejection of his heritage as a declaration of its inadequacy to satisfy the rather ambiguous yearnings of the post-war generation. Stimulated by his contact with the teeming city and the novelty of his circumstances of West Egg, Nick gives in to a most compelling illusion.(Steinbrink 160)

Robert Ornstein observers, "Gatsby is a story of 'displaced persons who have journeyed Eastward in search of larger experience of life." Further he goes on to say, "To Fitzgerald ...the lure of the East represents a profound displacement of the American dream, a turning back upon itself of the historic pilgrimage towards the frontier which had in fact, created and sustained that dream. In Gatsby the once limitless western horizon is circumscribed by the bored, sprawling, swollen towns beyond the Ohio."(Ornstein 63)

The East, where Gatsby sees the green light, inspires in him a romantic hope of orgiastic future. But it only shatters his dream and leads to his violent end. The East Egg appears attractive as "the city seen for the first time, in its wild promise of all the mystery and beauty in the world." But it appears so only from a distance and when one goes near, it is seen to be an "unreal city" with "ash-grey men who move dimly and already crumbling through the powdery air.(Steinbrink 163)

It is important to note that Gatsby is not destroyed by his bootlegging and the under-world connections. Coming from the West, he is unable to comprehend the materialistic ethic of the East. Daisy's selfishness and Tom's hard malice lead to the murder of Gatsby. Gatsby, whose romantic belief is firmly rooted in the ability to repeat the disembodied past, utterly fails to see through the falsity of the present. Though he is faintly aware that each step towards the green light is going to make the romantic glow less bright, he persists in his efforts towards attaining his goal, namely, winning Daisy. Even as the story reaches its climax and culminates in the violent death of Gatsby, Fitzgerald, in a highly poetic language, suggests Gatsby's essential connection with the West which represents his simplicity of heart and his romantic dream.(Callahan 381)

Gatsby carries on the spirit of romantic wonder of those Dutch sailors as Nick carrawy descripes Gatsby in the end of the novel, but the time and place are against him, and they turn the romantic promises of the future an illusory reflection of the past. However, we cannot say that Fitzgerald totally approved of the West or totally condemned the East. In fact, *The Great Gatsby* goes beyond the appraisals like the contemporary decadence of the East or the pristine virtues of the West.

According to Veronica Makowsky F. Scott Fitzgerald initially intended for his novel to have the title Among the Ash-heaps and Millionaires which would suggest that the author saw the issue of class as an important theme in the novel. Ash-heaps refers to the area of ashes where for instance the Wilsons live as well as other member of the working class. This area is a great contrast to that of the fashionable East Egg where the Buchanans and other members of the upper class live (Makowsky 75).

Throughout the story Gatsby is in pursuit of a dream. There are many claims for what that dream represents among scholars as well as readers, the most common ones being the love of Daisy Buchanan and the American dream. The concept of the American dream is closely related to the notion of class and although the American dream will not be the main focus of this thesis it will be dealt with to some extent. The American dream is a much wider concept than class and was, according to Therése Johansson's thesis: The Broken Dream, originally an expression describing the wish for a better life among the people who migrated to America. Later on it would include aspirations towards a better life for those already living in America as well (Therése 2).

Gatsby has a romantic view of wealth and is unaware of the realities of the American society where wealth is not the only aspect when it comes to social class (Bewley 28). There is a bond stronger than money between people like Tom and Daisy Buchanan and even though Gatsby has made a great fortune it is not enough to belong to the same social class as Tom and Daisy. Tom and Daisy's contempt against people like Gatsby, wealthy people but with a different socioeconomic background, is demonstrated by Daisy's loathing of West Egg, where Gatsby lives. This contempt as well as the bond between Tom and Daisy Buchanan can be explained with their similar upbringing and education. That is also evidence that no matter how hard Gatsby tries, he cannot change his past and he cannot change other people's past. Since status is, more than social class, dependent on things from the past, such as upbringing, it is also more difficult to change.

> About Gatsby! No, I haven't. I said I'd been making a small investigation of his past.""And you found he was an Oxford man," said Jordan helpfully."An Oxford man!" He was incredulous. "Like hell he is! He wears a pink suit."(Fitzgerald 66)

On the surface The Great Gatsby might seem to be a tragic love story between the golden girl and a poor young soldier going to war. The main theme of the novel however operates on a much larger scale and it would be a mistake not to recognize it. The novel offers a story of a whole generation. It is a story of a whole era, the Jazz era. Throughout American history the 1920s have always been referenced to as the golden age. It was a time of prosperity and material excess. Everybody could achieve the American dream if they tried hard enough. It was also a time of incredible hope. The American dream suddenly became something that everybody strived for. Fitzgerald experienced his American dream also when he became an instant celebrity after the publication of his first novel. To some the 1920s seemed almost like a dream. It was a careless time of living like there is no tomorrow:

> They were careless people, Tom and Daisy- they smashed up things
> and creatures and then retreated back into their money or their vast
> carelessness or whatever it was that kept them together, and let other
> people clean up the mess they had made. (Fitzgerald 98)

However the dream has been corrupted. Fitzgerald portrays the 1920s as a time of decayed social and moral values, time of greed and cynicism. People were interested only in pursuit of the material possessions and sexual pleasure. And it was all accompanied by the sound of the wild jazz music. After the war people returned haunted by the experience. They became the —Lost generation‖. Suddenly there was nothing more important than the gayety and enjoyment. This eventually led to the stock market crash in 1929.

With the two luxurious neighborhoods West Egg and East Egg Fitzgerald represents the divided society. The two Eggs, even though they might look alike, are different in behavior and values, which is demonstrated by the behavior of a few East Egg residents at a West Egg party: "Instead of rambling this party had preserved a dignified homogeneity, and assumed to itself the function of representing the staid nobility of the countryside – East Egg condescending to West Egg, and carefully on guard against its spectroscopic gayety" (Fitzgerald 47). Fitzgerald makes East Egg the symbol of the "old money" America that despises the "new money" America which is symbolized by West Egg. (Fälth 16)

With focus on their socioeconomic backgrounds, Fitzgerald makes clear examples of the typical residents of both East and West Egg. Tom and Daisy Buchanan are the typical residents of East Egg as they have always been wealthy and possess the freedom that comes with it. They are described as people that without any further purpose drift: "here and there unrestfully wherever people played polo and were rich together" (Fitzgerald 13). To them, there is nothing more to life than existing in this state of mind (Barbour 70). Gatsby, on the other hand, is the typical resident of West Egg. With his lack of family wealth and his self-earned fortune he represents the opposite from Tom and Daisy Buchanan. While the Buchanans seem to live without goals or ambition, Fitzgerald shows Gatsby's ambitions with the schedule over his daily activities (162).

Nick"s assertion several lines about the geographical thrust of the novel:

> "I see now that this has been the story of the West, after all—Tom and Gatsby, Daisy and Jordan and I, were all Westerners, and perhaps we possessed some deficiency in common which made us subtly unadaptable to Eastern life" (Fitzgerald 188).

Such a "deficiency" becomes easier to define when read against Nick"s observation that he had been made "a little complacent from growing up in the Carraway house in a city where dwellings are still called through decades by a family's name" (ibid188) and his earlier admission that after the war he returned to the Midwest "restless...Instead of being the warm center of the world the middle-west now seemed like the ragged edge of the universe" (5). (Reed 58)

The frontier having long passed it by, the Midwest for Nick now represents comfort and its dangerous twin, complacency. As the narrative has progressed, every major character flaw Nick observes in others has at its root a sense of complacency and stagnation. The Wilsons and the other denizens of the Valley of Ashes are stuck on 58 the short cut from nothing to nothing, Tom and Daisy are content to exist within their money and carelessness, and Gatsby has wed his "unutterable vision" to Daisy"s "perishable breath." In each case, forward momentum is surrendered, and with it a claim to American identity.

Notably, though, Nick says "this has been a story of the West" instead of the established term "middle-west" that he has used throughout the text. Such a lexical substitution recalls Gatsby"s own placement of San Francisco in the Midwest, for Nick, Gatsby"s "power to mobilize geographic and political boundaries" and which therefore implies that the boundaries of identity have become unfixed along with their geographical counterparts (Marren 94). Viewed through the twin lenses of history and ideology, such geographic substitution gains even more weight because by conflating the West and Midwest as geographical regions, Nick is also calling up associations with the individualistic pioneers. While the Midwest may be the "warm center of the world," it was once the frontier, and Nick wants to reclaim that frontier spirit, to revert the region to the "ragged edge of the universe" as a way of combating what he understands to be a threatening stasis. In other words, just as Dan Cody, the only representative of the "real" West in the book, once "brought back to the eastern seaboard the savage violence of the frontier brothel and saloon" Nick brings his and Gatsby"s story back to the Midwest in order to partake of its erstwhile vitalizing power (Turner 106).

As Fitzgerald points out through Nick's observations, the American dream used to be symbolized with discovery, individualism and the pursuit of happiness. However the relaxed and frivolous atmosphere of the 1920s has corrupted the dream. It has become synonymous with materialistic values, greed and immoral behavior. Gatsby's dream of loving Daisy is at first met with obstacles because they come from different social backgrounds and he can't offer her what she is used to. Later when he finally achieves material success and stability, Daisy is no longer available. That is the sad irony of Gatsby's dream:

> Gatsby believed in the green light, the orgastic future that year by year recedes before us. It eluded us then, but that's no matter — tomorrow we will run faster, stretch out our arms farther. . . . And one fine morning —— So we beat on, boats against the current, borne back ceaselessly into the past. (GG,2005, p. 183)

The premise of the American dream is that if you work hard enough to get something you will succeed. What he and other characters fail to realize is that the dream is just an illusion. Gatsby in a way embodies the American dream. He comes from nothing and becomes somebody. He has a desire and motivation to get his girl back but like many times before in the history he falls short of his dream.

Fitzgerald is very clever with placing his symbols and motifs. He interconnects them and so everything in the novel seems to have a deeper meaning. The green light is not just a light at the end of the dock. It is a symbol of the American dream. But while Gatsby symbolizes it with Daisy because she is his ultimate dream, Nick is able to connect it to American past.((Píchová pp.33,34))

The belief that American youth are subjected to neither rigid sitting nor heavy lifting is a convenient, class-specific fiction, and Nick"s counterposing Gatsby against both reveals his investment in elaborating on familiar notions of the American spirit. Both images recall ideas of rigid European caste systems, with sitting evoking the boarding school education reserved for the aristocracy and lifting standing in for the drudgery in store for everyone else. Likewise, both rigid sitting and lifting work suggest structure and oppression, with heavy loads literally weighing down the carriers and sitting representing absences of both play and movement. To this end, the correlation between this passage and Fredrick Jackson Turner"s (1920) frontier thesis—another piece heavily investing in defining a sense of the American character—is striking. (Turner 37)

The argument for inherited decency as a justification for limiting status change, however, is undercut almost immediately by the looming presence of Tom Buchanan, who, as even the most casual reader knows, is far from decent. In analyzing of Tom's character, tom embodies the decadence of the upper classes and so can be read as Fitzgerald's critique not of wealth person—but of non-productive wealth.(Lena 10)

It is important to note, however, that while the true Carraway family narrative echoes traditional notions of the self-made man (building up a business from scratch) and thus could be told in terms of the value of hard work, Nick emphasizes instead the element of passing (the substitute).7 While associating the Carraway story with the American narrative of hard work seems to add legitimacy, it doesn"t solve the problem of stasis because, as Nick"s trip trough the Valley of Ashes makes clear, hard work doesn"t necessarily lead to progress. According to John Hilgart in has effectively argued for a reading of the Valley of Ashes as a "history of material relations, moving from agricultural „ridges and hills" of „wheat" to a factory town of „chimneys and rising smoke," to the final dehumanized image of masses of indistinguishable men „who move dimly and crumbling through the powdery air"" (Hilgart 97)

References

1-Emma ,Johansson. *Old Money versus New:Class Identity as a Motivational Force in The Great Gatsby*.linnuas university

2-Joanna Stolarek. *"THE BEAUTIFUL AND THE DAMNED"—THE INFLUENCE OF ZELDA FITZGERALD ON F. SCOTT FITZGERALD'S LIFE AND LITERARY OUTPUT* .In .Muses, Mistresses and Mates. Creative Collaborations in Literature, Art and Life, Edited by Izabela Penier & Anna Suwalska-Kołecka *Newcastle upon Tyne: Cambridge Scholars Publishing.* Oct 2013 pp. 51-59

3- Michaela Píchová. *Comparative Analysis of Two Czech translations of Francis Scott Fitzgerald's The Great Gatsby*. Czech: Masaryk University,2014.

4-Robert Ornstein, "Scott Fitzgerald's Fable of East and West," *A Collection of critical essays,* ed. Kenneth Eble 63.

5-Jeffrey Steinbrink Source "Boats Against the Current": Mortality and the Myth of Renewal in The Great GatsbyAuthor(s):: Twentieth Century Literature, Vol. 26, No. 2, F. Scott Fitzgerald Issue (Summer,), New York,: Hofstra University, 1980. pp. 157-170

6-John ,F. Callahan. *F. Scott Fitzgerald's Evolving American Dream: The "Pursuit of Happiness" in Gatsby, Tender Is the Night, and The Last Tycoon.* Hofstra University, 1996.

7- Sebastian Fälth. *Social Class and Status in Fitzgerald's The Great Gatsby.* Sweden: Halmstad University,2013.

8- Barbour, Brian M. "Two American Dreams in Conflict". Johnson 72-67.

9- Johansson, Thérése. *The Broken Dream: The Failure of the American Dream in The Grapes of Wrath from a Caste and Class perspective.* Linnaeus University, 2010.

10-Makowsky, Veronica. "Among the Ash-heaps and Millionaires." *Approaches to teaching Fitzgerald's The Great Gatsby.* Ed. Jackson R. Bryer & Nancy P. VanArsdale. New York: Modern Language Association of America, 2009. 75-83.

11-Bewley, Marius. *Scott Fitzgerald"s Criticism of America.*" 1954. The Great Gatsby: A Study. Ed. Frederick J. Hoffman. New York: Scribner"s, 1962.

12-JEREMY REED.THE AMERICAN DREAM AND THE MARGINS IN TWENTIETH CENTURY FICTION. Columbia: University of Missouri,2009.print

13-Marren, Susan Marie. "Passing for American: Establishing American Identity in the Work of James Weldon Johnson, F. Scott Fitzgerald, Nella Larsen, and Gertrude Stein." Diss., University of Michigan, 1995. Print.

14-Lena, Alberto. "Deceitful Traces of Power: An Analysis of the Decadence of Tom Buchanan in The Great Gatsby." Canadian Review of American Studies. 28 (1998): 19-42. Web. 28 July 2005.

15-Turner, Fredrick Jackson. The Frontier in American History. New York: H. Holt and Company, 1920. Print.

16- Tom, Burnam. The Eyes of Dr. Eckleburg: A Re-Examination of "The Great Gatsby. Englewood Cliffs : Prentice Hall,1963. P 9

YOUR KNOWLEDGE HAS VALUE